NIKI HURTZ

Mood Swingin

Pieces of My Mind

First published by HVOE MEDIA 2021

Copyright © 2020 by Niki Hurtz

All rights reserved. No part of this publication may be reproduced, stored or transmitted in any form or by any means, electronic, mechanical, photocopying, recording, scanning, or otherwise without written permission from the publisher. It is illegal to copy this book, post it to a website, or distribute it by any other means without permission.

First edition

Contents

Preface	v
WHO IS NIKI HURTZ	1
TOO SOON	8
BROKEN SMILE	10
SURREAL	12
TO MOMMY, WITH LOVE	14
NEVER BETTER	17
UNDERSTANDING LONELINESS	18
QUID PRO QUO	20
MISCONCEPTION	22
BURIAL	23
COMBAT	25
WRONG SIDE OF RIGHT	27
CHICK'N	31
TRAUMATIC	32
REGRET	35
DEEP SHIT	37
HELP	42
REPEAT OFFENSE	43
EPIPHANY	44
PARENT TRAPPED	45
FAMILY TREE	47
FLOWERS	48
ROTTEN GRAPEVINE	49

DEPRESSION	54
EMOTIONLESS	57
FAREWELL	59
DON'T JUDGE ME	60
HER	62
LOSE CONTROL	63
MISS, I'M PRETTY	64
REALITY SUCKS	66
HAPHAZARDLY ESTRANGED	67
PROPHETIC	70
TALES OF THE HOOD	72
KILL THEM BEFORE THEY GROW	74
QUICKSAND	78
RECONCILIATION	82

Preface

Mood Swingin' has been a long time coming. Over the years of conceptualizing, it has taken many forms and I have felt so many different emotions about what each of those changes meant for me and my book baby. We have come full circle to our original format, a book of poetry.

Poetry became a coping mechanism for me as a young child, reading poetry was like discovering magic and when I learned that I could write it, I spared not one moment. Carefully crafted messages, synthesized rhyme patterns and pregnant pauses that were filled with imagery became the means by which I expressed what was happening down on the inside of me. I lived with depression and anxiety for most of my life and while I often found myself at a loss for words to describe my thoughts and feelings, writing poetry offered an outlet that I can honestly say was life saving.

I was an adult before I could completely appreciate the solace that poetry offered. It was not until after my 19th birthday when I penned one of my most personal pieces, *Who is Niki Hurtz*, that I gained a true appreciation for the therapeutic art of poetry. The release that I felt after I completed that piece was priceless. That release opened up a new world for me. It never solved a problem for me, I want to make that perfectly clear, but what it did do was offer me a clean perspective on what I was feeling internally.

Mood swingin was my norm. My emotions were always unpredictable yet extremely deliberate. Everything that I felt was extreme; extreme excitement, extreme anger, extreme sadness, I'd run the gamut of extreme feelings. I didn't understand why I felt so hard and often the subject matter left me even more puzzled.

Herein lies thirty-seven works bred by first and second hand experiences that helped to shape my understanding of the ebb and flow of life. Through this understanding I was able to gain even more clarity about my own thoughts, feelings and beliefs. The imperfection of life can make or break you, because imperfection by definition is undesirable. Its in those moments of gross undesirability that one must make a choice, do I give in or do I fight?

LET'S GET READY TO RUMBLE...

WHO IS NIKI HURTZ

Niki
That's me
Niki
You'll see
They say
She's strong
I am
Some say
She's wrong
I could be

That's Niki
I'm me

They say
She's deep
That's me
Some say
She's crazy
Think I could be?

I'm irreplaceable

MOOD SWINGIN

That's what I am
Don't like
Can't appreciate my words?

I don't give a damn
There's the door
Close it!
I'm not through with you yet
You owe me your attention
You leave now
that's an unpaid debt

I'm Niki
that's me
I walk through fires
And on the floor of the sea
Beat down doors with my bare fists
Don't charge no fee
I could be your superwoman if you want me to be

No I couldn't
I could just be me
That's Niki
I'm me

I stand up at times
When most are afraid
Stage sit ins
When I've a point
That needs to be made
Won't let you walk all over me

WHO IS NIKI HURTZ

Nah not today
Cuz by any means necessary
I'ma get paid

I'm a black woman
In a white ruled world
Some don't consider me a woman
Merely a young girl
So tell me
Am I the confused one
in this ragged world?

Anyway tell me this
How young is pain?
You know that stabbing feeling
Then it's never the same?
You know the one when your world crumbles
And you don't know who to blame?

From what I'm understanding
Pain doesn't have an age

See
I called the cops and told them how pain raped me with rage
Grabbed me from behind by my braids
Inserted
and proceeded to pound like he was on center stage

And I was helpless as pain pounded away
Arched my back

MOOD SWINGIN

and then mounted my neck
Pushed all the way back and
I knew what was next

When pain got weak
I began to cry tears
He seemed satisfied
that to heals his wounds would take years

Just when I thought it was over
Misery smiled at me
She sucked on my mounds
And shoved them at me
She went on down
To lick on my wound
The way that it burned
I knew that pain
had swelled it up like a balloon.
She turned around and
She sat on my face
Pain holding my tongue
made me lick her wounded place

When it was over
Misery slipped me her number
Said she needed a friend

Anyway
Since that day
I've been trying to tell my story
No one seems to understand

WHO IS NIKI HURTZ

But I know it's not just for me

That's Niki
I'm me
I'm human
I feel
I bleed
I cry
Niki Hurtz
And I don't know why

I don't suffer from any disorders
Just misunderstanding
And I don't need your quarters to go in my can
And, I don't want for you to sympathize with me.
Just take the time to listen and get to know me

Don't tell me that my wounds will heal
And that pain don't last always
Cuz he might not stay forever
But he's around for more than a day

Every Night he comes to stick it in
And remind me that he's there
And he's never alone
Misery comes too
Because she's a friend who cares

So don't try to comfort me
and make me feel better
I just want to show you who I am

MOOD SWINGIN

for those who've never met her

I'm Niki
I'm me
I'm human
I feel
I bleed
I cry

Niki Hurtz
And I don't know why
Niki Hurtz
When You walk on by
Niki Hurtz
Every time you lie

Niki,
That's me
I hope you see
How I'm strong
I'm wrong
I'm deep
And I'm crazy

Pain don't last always but every night he comes and rapes me
Misery loves company
I'm her best friend
We both sleep in skirts
Pain comes
Does his thing
And Niki Hurtz

WHO IS NIKI HURTZ

Need I say it again?

TOO SOON

You left too soon for us
instead of dancing with us
you are now dancing with the angels

Traces of you appear
with tear stricken smiles
echoes of your laughter
memories of your style
the scent of your perfume
and warm embraces
holds us in your shadow
you left too soon

He wanted you home
His reason
His own
but He wanted you home

In our daily lives
we know that you're with us
whether on smooth road
or bucking through ditches

TOO SOON

in our hearts you appear
in our smiles you shine
not one ounce of love
did you leave behind

You bore from your womb
a new generation
taught to respect themselves and life
never asking for much glory in your name
I've seen you cry a million tears and never once complain
money didn't make you rich
but love is all you know
being all and given this
you had a heart of gold

Now though you've taken
your long walk to the golden stair
we'll always know you're with us
through the suns golden glare

BROKEN SMILE

What happened to my little girl?
Someone broke her smile
I miss those teeth shining like pearls
haven't seen them in a while

Someone stole her twinkle
They broke the sparkle in her eyes
I can hardly recognize the girl
whose eyes were once
big, innocent and shy

It was deeper than a heartbreak
and even stronger than some lies
Damage so deep
results are clearly physically described

Spirit breaking evil
riddled with even more sin
Callously denying the status
as it's always been

Covered up with mud

BROKEN SMILE

in the spirit of a bad name
A legacy of which she has no control
from which hence she came

Someone stole her happy
Whole world shattered
filled with shame
An identity crisis
only recognizable by name

SURREAL

She was just a young girl
Who was mad at her mother
Couldn't understand her father
With plans to free her sister and brother

She sat at the train
racing thoughts
heavy heart
no plans to turn back
no clue where to start

She returned to a place
Familiar from birth
That she frequented often
Now reclaimed as her turf

Sponging up quickly
What she'd need to survive
No guts, no glory
And no place to hide

As the story would go

SURREAL

She was all alone
Equipped with the strength
and the need
To make her own home

But her mother was dead
and her sperm donor had been gone
And the father that she knew
Well the conclusion was drawn
That she was too big for her britches
and maybe just as well gone

She was just a child
who needed immediate help
Everyone from whom she sought it
cared more about their ego
than her emotional health.

Void of support
She'd struggle for real
Emotional exile
A hard swallowed pill
And she was a stepchild
For the first time she'd feel
Like she never really mattered

It was all so surreal

TO MOMMY, WITH LOVE

At night
I awake drenched in sweat
And for a moment
It's like I forget
No matter what the memories
My cries overcome the laughter
Remembering your last smiles and fun
Then remembering
why none came thereafter
Thoughts and feelings of loneliness
engulf me
Time and time again
To the naked eye
I'm fine and quiet
But my cries
are held within

There are those around me
Who sense there's something wrong
When rather than tears of sorrow
Anger arises
and forces its stay to prolong

TO MOMMY, WITH LOVE

Then there are those
Who think I'm quite alright
They either fail to realize
Or don't want to see that
Silence brutalizes my fight

Losing you
I lost half of me
My very very best friend
And while time spent was precious
All the way up until the end
There are a few things
that I want to share with you
Because I've grown

Now that I've ventured
Out on my own
I can fully appreciate
Your insight and wisdom
All of those words
I didn't want to hear before
Truth be told I kind of miss them

And after spreading my wings
And realizing all that
Life may bring
I've offered my bosom to the world
and learned
To forgive, love, and feel

I know I'm beginning to ramble

MOOD SWINGIN

but there's so much I need to cover
Most of all you should know
That I miss you mother

I'll place these words
on the wings of a dove
And hope that it reaches you

To Mommy, with Love

NEVER BETTER

Hello

Do you remember me?

I'm the adult version of the little girl
that you never cared to see

I'm the bastard child who dreamed
that it would be all good
that you'd eventually be present
and make your absence understood

I'm the angry woman
unable to let go of my past

The first man that was supposed to love me
fell way short
he set a tone
and I knew he wouldn't be the last

UNDERSTANDING LONELINESS

Can daddy's status
determine how we love in life?
Can daddy turn me
from a whore to a housewife?

When I search for love
do I want it there?
Or would I rather daddy?
Just someone to care

When lovers look at me
do they see love?
Or just a gullible little girl
who will adjust to fit any glove?

When I hurt
do I hurt in vain?
Or do I hurt to share the scars
created by my pain?

When I cry for comfort
daddy

should it be?
Or just the likes of any man holding me?

When I say forgive me
am I inviting you
to overlook my faults?
The same thing I should do

When I stand alone
is it by choice or chance?
Or does loneliness from the beginning
affect my permanent stance?

QUID PRO QUO

I know you didn't listen
I doubt you even cared
Those times you let me go
just so that your time was spared

I can bet that you were having fun
while it was me
I was his chosen one

I was the only one

But to you that never mattered
Picked up or dropped off
either way you scattered

I knew you never wanted me
I tried to tell you so
But to you perception's everything
So you didn't wanna know

You were only ever consistent
in trying to stop my glow

QUID PRO QUO

it pained me more than anything
that you didn't want to see me grow
and you never had to say the words
its all your actions show

Can't share my experience
birth parent but even so
I know in public you'll feign anger
and in private urge me to let it go

So I hold it close and tight
its the chip on my shoulder
but what would you know
we don't have a relationship of healing
its more of quid pro quo

MISCONCEPTION

You tell me that you love me
but the only time you touch me
is when your fist is in my eye
You say you'll never leave me
but never hesitate to say goodbye
I question if it's over
Should we give another try
You fuck me and leave me there
harboring another lie

BURIAL

How can I sit here
and really pretend?
How can I perpetrate?
I know it's more than just a friend

But meanwhile
Fuck all that
You don't deserve my tears
I've had no real reason
to cry in years

Thinkin you're gonna
be the one to open up my tear ducts
Your sadly mistaken

Don't come to breakfast
I made grits
with the eggs and turkey bacon

Take the bus today
I mean
I'm just guessin

MOOD SWINGIN

But you might wanna take your car
to get an inspection

Don't wear those shoes
the lightbulb
had broke in the closet

I don't really wanna harm you
so
let me just stop it
Just know that I'm through

Don't got no time
nor patience
to be playing games with you

So fuck you for life
Screw you for living
This shit has been dead
I'm just finished digging

COMBAT

Pain was my daily
so I thought that was love

Assorted methods of branding
could be indicative of
a passionate connection
that romance authors write of
or a visual perception
of a lack of self love

A regular slugger
southpaw for the win
anytime the left foot went back
no doubt
the left fist would come in

And the counterattack
quick jab
hook
gets me in
but he quickly gets back
and continues as he's been

MOOD SWINGIN

because his manhood long ago
died of chagrin

And my pride died too
cuz I knew it was wrong
but I felt stuck
after I had put up with it for so long
like in a rut
down on my luck
and I like to think that I'm strong
but what the fuck
there was a glut
of reasons I should've moved on

WRONG SIDE OF RIGHT

I had to give up on him
Thinking of him
Kept me up all night
But I loved him
With all of myself
I'd just
had enough tonight

I couldn't quite think
Of what he did to keep me
except leave me
with a lumped head
and black eyes
Whatever it was
he pleased me
Silenced my sweet sorrows
and sad goodbyes

He loved me like I never felt
Purposely
As if he understood
The pain I felt within myself

MOOD SWINGIN

and the remedy to make me feel good

There was a condom missing from the box
We hadn't used one in ages
Lipstick circled his collar
I only wore that on special occasions
And it was never the bright red
that shown on his once white shirt
Nor was that my scent
rising from his slacks

Yet he laid in my bed
Like it was all good
And left me to sleep
with his back
I tried to reason with him
but that would never matter
The blood he left
the last time he broke my heart
muted any senseless chatter
I dreaded sleep
and worshipped pain
Wondered how I'd
get through it again

The sleepless nights
meaningless chatter
The fast life
senseless clatter
The aromatic drugs
Emotionless sex

WRONG SIDE OF RIGHT

I had come to the end of my world
and couldn't think of what was next

Forever I'd been stuck
in a personal prison
Barb-wired fence
and no supervision
A dangerous combination
See
I was secretly suicidal
but could never find the heart to harm myself

I dreaded going back
to the prison
where there was no one there
No one to lean on
Nor anyone who'd pretend to care
Wondered why I couldn't appreciate myself
Worship myself for the person that I am
Why I took the credit from myself
Denied myself any real glam

Any blind man could see
that I was unhappy
My drug abuse was out of hand
and my self-esteem
crappy

This time,
I vowed to myself
that things would be different

MOOD SWINGIN

No more powdered appetizers
served in makeshift dishes

I stared at his back
crossed my fingers real tight
Closed my eyes
saw the condom box
My courage gained a lil height
thought of scrubbing the lipstick stain
This would be my last night
The stench coming from his slacks
Put my target in sight

I stared at his back
Told my sorrows goodnight
...woke up in the morning
reach for my mirror and straw
Here I go again
On the wrong side of right

CHICK'N

Early this morning
bout an hour before he woke—
I let him know
that I'd be better on my own
I didn't wake him
I just left a note

TRAUMATIC

Trauma changes you
Well I feel
unhealthy and untamed
disfigured
no part of me is the same
Incapacitated
its hard to move through the pain
Duplicated
its happened time after time
and again

Too trusting
because I thought it was all good
Disgusting
completely inebriated I stood
Groove busting
suddenly,
not feeling so good

Did you know what was gonna go down?
was it between you and your bro
consecrated by a shake or a pound.

TRAUMATIC

I ask because
you were mighty quick to judge
I'm just saying
did you know that he would
take a bathroom break with delay
and...

So no one questioned where he went?
No one worried about my safety
or how much time that he spent?

Blinded by meaningless connections
and unrequited love
light speed
that's how quick your role changed
turned co-conspirator to the fuzz

I was fucked up
but I wasn't asleep
Blacked out from the fill of my system
I fell victim to the creep

Violated
my drunken strength
no match for his conniving ways
Suddenly sober
shock and paralysis
there was that phase
I can't believe...

Eyes open

MOOD SWINGIN

look down
completely astounded
the human form
of the new, improved me
No longer drunken
but oh how I've sunken
so much
its too damn hard to see

I don't even recognize me
multiple assaults in a matter of hours
both emotionally and physically
quizzically
all eyes are on me cynically
I'm questioning what's gotten into you
because you can't believe what he did to me

REGRET

Sometimes I wish
that I could travel backwards through time
Choices I made would be different
Putting my soul at peace
as well as my mind

Wouldn't say
I wish I never met you
just should've been more careful

Preservation of your feelings
Came before attraction
Maybe the preservation
caused a backup
Cuz what came next was a chained reaction

Events and words
that should've never taken place
My careful planning
preserved the look of shock upon your face

When I said goodbye

MOOD SWINGIN

    We're through
  I don't really like girls
Just said that to get away from you

DEEP SHIT

Help me out
help me move
help me breathe
Grab me
Cuz right now
I'm going down
on bended knee

And I don't
wanna do it
but I gotta do it
Cuz you put me through it
it's
so
deep

Deeper than the ocean's
number one love potion
turn the wheels in motion
Cuz I just want you

Right our wrongs

MOOD SWINGIN

blend our feelings
not conform
this affair
has run long
but I don't want it to be gone
go deep

Right now I'm waking up
with teary eyes
no answer to the question
that I'm constantly asking
why?
Why did I take this path
why we move this fast
why can't this thing last
Go deep

You should've walked away
boy your playing a dangerous game
I don't know what to say
it's foul how you running game

Cuz this could get so deep
between me and you
I could dig so deep
for what I went through
this could get real deep
if you want it to
Pack your shit
cuz I ain't got no rap for you

DEEP SHIT

Desperate for love
disgustingly naive
I thought my back shot
would be the reason
you'd never leave
the way I ride dick
would be the reason
you'd never cheat
my head game was vicious
sure to keep you
between the sheets

But it was pussy by the dozens
that was keeping you
in the street
no matter how I fucked ya
cuz you wanna
you gonna creep
wouldn't be surprised
another bitch soiled my sheets
remember when I tell you
this can get
real deep

This could get so deep
between me and you
I could dig so deep
for what I been through
this could get real deep
if you want it to
Pack ya shit cuz

MOOD SWINGIN

I ain't got no rap for you

Gave all I could
to cater to you
can't say that I
expected faithful from you
exclusive would do
but without a clue
you left me with
your work and constant reminders of you
conveniently you stopped through
so we could do what we do
quickly returning to the streets
to see who else you could screw

And I was waiting for you
sitting here patient for you
as you took time
deciding who'd be
home station for you
I don't know what you gon do
As long you know I'm through
Your work
fell in the toilet
Got a plunger for you
Oooppps

Deeper than relations
and you saving face
and tryna stay complacent
cuz I don't want you

DEEP SHIT

I was wrong
your dick is really long
its in me
then its gone
now my feelings not as strong
go deep

Don't wanna see you
so I close my eyes
don't wanna hear
what you're saying
cuz its probably
all lies
I'm on to your ass
pack your shit and fast
this ain't gonna last

HELP

Please pay attention
please notice what's going on
I can barely keep from crying
like a stranger's in our home
Please tell me the truth
don't shun me with omission and lies
I love you more than anything
but won't hesitate to say goodbye
Or maybe I will
I'm barely sleeping or can't you tell?
My mood is completely unstable
but you wouldn't notice
you think I like to yell
Please pay attention
Please notice what's going on
I can barely keep from crying
there's a stranger in our home

REPEAT OFFENSE

Placed my pride to the side
To explain the tears upon my face
Repeated signs of nonchalance
Placed me in this wounded space

My heart is heavy with hurt
tears competing in my eyes
I'd rather cry goodbye
Than due to your selfish pride

To you my pain is stupid
To me that's not the case
For I've pleaded with you many times
While tears ran down my face

To you it doesn't matter
To me that is just fine
Just carry yourself toward the door
And leave me behind

EPIPHANY

Asked to borrow my time
And changed my mind completely
What I thought I never wanted
swept me off my feet
and beat me
Never touching nor tasting
Beyond accidental grazes
I frowned at the thought
of just going thru phases

On a regular basis
This all wouldn't matter
But you've snapped me back to reality
and my dreams aren't shattered

PARENT TRAPPED

Gentle yet stern
loving always
supportive beyond measure
parenthood is far from a phase
it's a silent pact made
to surrender the rest of your days
obsessing over the unconditional love
just for you that God made

Parenthood does not care
if you're tired or weary
it's only concern is
the child who loves you so dearly
it's homework checked daily
and dinner cooked nightly
it's maintaining diplomacy
even when behavior deviates slightly
it's cleaning fresh wounds
and comforting broken hearts
no guidebook exists
nor a button to restart

MOOD SWINGIN

Its in your best interest
to cherish each moment as they come
the role is ever changing
and as they grow older they run

FAMILY TREE

Divide and grow
generation after generation
that's all we know
division and growth
few know the story of how we got here
but no one stays close

The tree has branched off in many directions
flush cut branches, collars and the lateral sections
From the branches would many fruit grow
mindlessly neglecting where they come from
and due to division they'd never know

FLOWERS

If you are not careful
one day you will look up
and they will be gone

There will be no fanfare
no final call

Life changes in an instant
and a change for one is a change for all
It is a one act play
unscripted improv
no intermission

Give them their flowers while they're here
truer words have never been spoken
because once their gone
all that's left is hope when
It didn't have to be that way

Now you're left with regret
and the words you never did say

ROTTEN GRAPEVINE

I heard that you were gone
I heard that through the grapevine
They told me that you'd left
And that was just fine
Until
They told me that you were gone for good
Six feet under
And I begged
Please somebody knock on wood

It was over street games
You had earned your street fame
Had a gun
With a clip
And a good ass aim
The white man's to blame
Well at least that's what you said
But if the white man's to fault
Why are all my black kings dead?

You were sellin that shit
That shit that you knew could kill

MOOD SWINGIN

Walkin round grabbin your dick
Yellin
I'm keepin it real

Real?
Well you're not anymore
Can't look forward to you
knockin at my door
The game you played had one rule
And that was to watch your back
When asked about your front and sides
You told me you had everything in tact

I begged for you to stop
But you just kept on goin
And in your game plan
I became one of your pawns
So if the enemy attacked
I was in the line of fire
But that was no matter to you
Cuz you just took the game higher

I had to move to away
and separate myself from you
But before I left
I told you exactly what I'd do
I said I'd call you after work
and pray for you every night and day
But now I'm praying for your soul
Because your body's gone astray

ROTTEN GRAPEVINE

Cops found you ass out
in the trunk of a Chromed out Navigator
with a message on your pager reading
Nigga I'll catch you later

Your mom,
She didn't find out until the next day
That her only son was gone
God had taken him away
She wailed and yelled
And even damned your daddy to hell

She fell to the floor
with the claim that it was her fault
She wanted to die
as she lay there distraught
She refused to eat
And cried herself to sleep
Her only baby was gone
And she herself
no longer felt strong

Your girl,
she didn't find out for days
Two days had gone by
and you didn't return her page
And she called your mom
and she told her you were gone
She fell to her knees
and cried on the floor
How could she tell Jahniece

MOOD SWINGIN

that her daddy was gone?
Would she ever understand
that her daddy was wrong?
Would she ever remember
their two short spent years?
Would she ever understand
her mommy's tears?

She moved away
And she remembered you
And she made sure Jahniece
knew of you too
Never
Could she let your memory pass
But if only as your memory
Your life would've lasted

Me?
Back to me
I'm angry with you
I thought
When I graduated
you'd be there too
You said on my prom
You would go
and you promised together
we would show
A platonic friendship
between boy and girl

But now I'll cry

ROTTEN GRAPEVINE

every night before I sleep
And I'll whine
as the pain cuts a lil too deep
I'm sorry
I couldn't be there
when they laid you under
Honestly
that night I thought there was thunder
Well I guess this is goodbye
but not yet the end
Cuz one day
Hopefully not too soon
I'll meet you in heaven my friend

DEPRESSION

I don't feel like doing my hair
And I don't give a damn how much you care
I mean what I say
I'm not doing my hair

I'm not changing my clothes
There's no way a new outfit will make me feel whole
Don't ask me again
I'm not changing my clothes

Just leave me alone
Let me be
You're way off
Trying to fix what you can't even see

It's so hard to change my mind
Nearly impossible to unwind
I appreciate your concern
But this happens all of the time

I'm not going outside
It's only hurting YOUR pride

DEPRESSION

I could care less what they think
They don't know how I feel inside
I'm not going outside

I'm tired
Tired of trying
tired of lying
tired of trying to figure out
if I'm dying

Tired of therapy
they got the best of me
cooperation is key
but they get no more out of me

Happiness seems so far away
and peace of mind won't ever let me stay
you're seeking an explanation
while I'm seeking the nearest freeway

Do you know what it's like to feel dead inside?
Watching everyone living
while your own living is implied
No matter how intricate the costume
It's never enough to disguise
the dead dark of night is the only place you can hide

Just leave me alone
Let me be
you're way off
trying to fix what you can't see

MOOD SWINGIN

I said it before
and I'll say it again
Hair, clothes and socializing
Can't fix what's within

I bid you farewell
adios
adieu
stay prayed up
don't let depression catch you

EMOTIONLESS

Dramatics to a minimum
Cuz silence is my venom
Hear they think I hit rock bottom
What I look like giving into them?
Confusion is the catalyst
Ignorance is defense to them
They're loathsome and their lying
Thinking that I need a cent from them

I struggle
but I can smell the success
There'll be quite a few periods
Through which I'll be in debt
Everything will be charged
And I'll come up way short
Its through these times it'll seem
as if I need support
But I need to be alone
to learn to take care of me
Trying to evolve from where I'm at
to where I wanna be

MOOD SWINGIN

Gotta use my own two
not on a lean always
And so I might seem very stubborn
as I go through my phase
Might get excited today
then tomorrow shy away
Gotta explore all of the aspects
Do this my way

So if it seems like I'm chillin
trust me I'm really dealing
with the pain and aggravation
I'm just good at concealing
What I'm thinking and feeling
cuz there's no use in killing
the mood of those around me
I'm no emotional villain

And out of no where
I'll come
You'll hear the beat of my drum
living my life
just how I always knew
that it should be done
Instead of work seems like fun
and I'll tell them all one by one
never underestimate someone
determined to not be outdone

FAREWELL

Everyday that I stay
Another part of me dies
With little sorrow in my heart
I tell the beliefs that birthed me
Goodbye
I've seen far too much here
and accomplished very little
And wisely I've realized
That to leave
is the only way
to find a happy middle

DON'T JUDGE ME

Some critic lady told me
She didn't like me
Couldn't stand
the way that I was
Told me I was nothing

She commented because
Someone told her
I was happy with mediocrity
She said that she felt bad
And would never want to be me

I find no fault
in the way I dance around
I just know that I'm a queen
awaiting my crown
Cuz I've got style and attitude
and live to be free

This critic lady stopped me
And said she didn't like me
Just because she wears

DON'T JUDGE ME

her business suits all of the time
Don't hardly make her job
no better than mine

I'm an aspiring artist
You'll soon hear of me
In the meantime
I do checkout
At the nearby grocery

HER

I put the itch in bitch
I mean I get under your skin
Got the meanest switch
And a chesire grin
straight edges like a garter stitch
I came to play and I play to win
I found my niche
forever feeding my future kin

Without much thought
I've moved on to what's next
Sandbagged all remorse
and abandoned regret
Shed my winter skin
Now I'm coming correct
Fuck being humble
I was born to flex

LOSE CONTROL

Doesn't matter your affliction
sick with selling crack to those with addiction
sick with playing whore to niggas on a mission
sick with sellin out the person who lives within
your true self
only turn to when you need help
hungry streets devour
those chasin money and power
scary ones will cower
and change they minds by the hour
cuz they can't grasp hold
of what it is they've consistently been told
its too late once the story unfolds
cuz you about to lose control

MISS, I'M PRETTY

She stood in line
waiting to be chosen
could've been ass naked
wasn't wearin no clothes and
there was no portfolio inside her hand
thought she was next top model
was desperate for fans

She argued with me
that she was well educated
demanded respect
and was not to be played with...

The director said ACTION
You'll never guess what happened

If she had a doctorate
it wouldn't mean much
cuz the cameraman had captured
nothin but her butt
and she cheesed shakin it
it cost her self respect

MISS, I'M PRETTY

and willingly she gave it

I wept for her cuz
she would be on BET representing me
a black woman
whether she liked it or not
she would be objectified
and known for dropping like its hot
it would be assumed
that she had gave him top
while he smacked on her bottom
a willing victim of sodom
me?

Not knockin shawty
but that's an image I'm not tryna see
might make him horny
he gon hit and treat you like a flea
thought you was different
but to them you're just another...
be yourself,
fight the pressure,
have some dignity

REALITY SUCKS

If I live in fear
I'll never get ahead
but asserting myself
could leave me dead
status has absolutely no standing in this matter
My brown skin tone
is the sole deciding factor

HAPHAZARDLY ESTRANGED

I am of a GREAT race
My men peruse
the plains of each country
In search
Of a life they think they've lost

Running
Like wild banshees
Some run away from themselves
They run
They run away from me
They flee

For my image shames them
I am
Constantly reminded of my skin
The color of plain earth
Rich in melanin
And for what it's worth
That's what protects me

I cause much shame

MOOD SWINGIN

With my homegrown features
Not the epitome of the motherland
But strong enough to be a keeper

From the thorny patch
Atop my head
To my hipstory
Outlined in red
Along the mountainous plains
Hung from my chest
Through my rambling mind
Employing duress

I represent a legacy
Disparaged from a deep rooted past
Saturated in pain
Exhausted
From being used
For other's personal gain
Foreign tongue
So they're confused
I protest
They call it complain

And in the midst of this
we forgot how strong we were
Lynched, chained, and whipped
we forgot how smart we were
Battles were never fist to fist
we lost the fight in us
And any bravery was stripped

HAPHAZARDLY ESTRANGED

there went the might in us

Shame
Became the remedy for pain
The theory of Willie Lynch persists
and continues to maim
It's easier to coexist
Than it is to declaim
What's been etched
in our psyche
So we cradle the blame

I am of a GREAT nation
Haphazardly estranged
Embedded in each constituent
Is the fight that's unexplained
Despite conceived differences
our struggles are quite the same
Different battles
Same war
The message doesn't change

PROPHETIC

And there he sat
with his gift in his lap
neatly wrapped in rhetoric
bow top center
to the back

I knew when my soul called for him
that I would have to help him grow
to find comfort in who's inside of him
and a way to let him show

Who he really is
He doesn't even know him
he's been in hiding since a kid
and if by chance he tried to emerge amid
the general public
he was quickly muzzled and hid

And so he sat
with his gift in his lap
eager to unwrap

PROPHETIC

I had to break it to him
he'd have to unlearn
before he could unpack
and from that moment forward
he could never go back

So he parted ways
with his limiting beliefs
shedding along the way
every time misunderstanding
brought him grief
every time his evolution
was met with resistance
when they built barriers for him
while he was offering relief

And there he sat
with his gift in his lap
secular abilities called into question
because he's on the right track
every time he takes a step forward
there are two steps to take back
but as long as he stays consistent
he'll make up for his slack

Now he stands
with his gift in his hand
no longer longing to unwrap
because now he understands
that his gift was not meant for him
but to serve others in the land

TALES OF THE HOOD

Tales of the hood
where by the time you learn good
the next generation wishes you would
dare try to deter them from the allures of the hood
standing tall on the same streets where you once stood

Its a cycle that's gotta end
cuz everytime it begins
A mother loses a child
and some lose a dear friend

Same movie
different cast
new ones determined to be
better than the last

If nothing changes
nothing changes
Old heads retire into danger
Young buls become just distant strangers

And if the narrative's unchanging

and the cycle remains untamed then
there's no moral to the story
and the mindset stays the same
The future looks so meek
as our present state maintains
Admirable legacy's been drained
We fail to rise above the trappings
unbroken cycle is sustained

KILL THEM BEFORE THEY GROW

Heartbreak like no other
When news of loss hits
There is not one of us
that is any different from the other
You're right
This time it wasn't me
But I've been there
Or maybe I haven't
Yet it still hurts to see
Your family and friends in pain
I swear if I could make it happen
We'd never experience it ever again

Especially the pain of loss
It's that pain you learn to live with
But you can't turn it off
When the funeral service is over
And you've paid up all costs
Your grief lasts forever
While sympathy exhausts

While most are trying to stifle it

KILL THEM BEFORE THEY GROW

I'm struggling to keep it aglow
I'm ecstatic for the success stories
But those aren't the ones that I know

When you watch the baby become a child
And the child become a teen
And as the years go by
You watch them choosing between
Which way to grow
Focused on the future or the moment
The gentleman or the schmo

Somebody's killing our babies,
Taking their chances away
Writing them off as if they shouldn't exist
They are expendable each of them

Preschoolers prosecuted in the form of suspension
Their ambition we may never know
A path lay paved for them
Before they were conceived
It's purpose
Kill them before they grow.

History whitewashed, twisted and maimed
Value debunked as if it doesn't exist
We've gone through kidnapping, slavery,
Revolts, desegregation and civil rights
Still it all boils down to this

Miseducation is the name of the game

MOOD SWINGIN

Indifference is their most famous claim to fame
Ignorant and simultaneously denying disdain
But get this
There's no denying, we're stained

It's like the mark of the beast
The melanin we can't cease
and they circle above us
like a vulture preying on its feast
constantly fighting the fear
of arrest or sudden decease
and so long as we are
unable to live at peace
our morale takes a steady decline
slope shows a major decrease

Discord in the community
To kill us we take equal opportunity
Defeating the credence of the agenda
with widespread disunity
Thinking they low
while most of us know
they use our culture
to push the wrong message
with untiring importunity
Immediate apathy outbreak
acquired through passive immunity

Head hunted
Growth stunted
Counted out and affronted

KILL THEM BEFORE THEY GROW

Coming of age in a land
where we were born to be Wanted
Somebody's killing our babies
and the weapons are flaunted
Expanding prisons and graveyards
cuz from birth they are taunted

QUICKSAND

Living fast and dying young
tell me
what oh what
have we become

Babies
Instead of preparing for SATs
we're hash tagging RIPs
trying to preserve
the short legacy
of the kid
with the big dreams
that they'll never get to see

And then there's little old me
trying to figure out what I can do
or how much help that I can be
because sometimes I feel like
I'm dying too
When as far as I can see
A generation eradicated
before their lives could even come to be

QUICKSAND

Families tormented with pain
friends afraid, lost and confused
no one will ever be the same
when it's the face that you love on the news
it doesn't matter who's to blame
the pain all feels the same

Another life cut short
presence missed
neighborhood in turmoil
residents concerned, scared and pissed

And what's it all over?
Some unregulated aggression
Ego inflated
til it's called into question
a decision that's made
to live up to perception

We're diseased in the mind
rampant moral infection
the issues we must deal with
are paramount before and after election
and instruction is needed
even when class is not in session

All over social media
our babies are stressing
brokenhearted emojis
to caption traumatic lessons
affect

MOOD SWINGIN

aggressive
because they're scared to show affection
they feel lost in the world
and don't trust the directions

And how can we blame them?
when "leadership" boasts their flexion
screaming from the mountain tops
but can't face their own reflection
and then there's the photo op
without any connection
their vulnerability exploited
for some selfish protections

We scream we need change
but don't make the connection
sending them up the river
coming down like advection
river current filled with pollution
that's bound to spread
like an untreated infection
not the change we needed
but he won the election

Meanwhile there's no programs
in our tattered section
and despite what good comes from here
it's overshadowed by imperfections
while our communities are marred by
mid level misdirection
so between the middle and the lower level

QUICKSAND

there's unprecedented disconnection

How can they assist where they don't understand?
When they choose to look the other way
as if these conditions aren't planned?
Using the diamond in the rough as the example
that should stand
when in reality its hard to dream
when it feels like you're standing in quick sand

RECONCILIATION

His daddy ain't never showed him nun
his mama wasn't worried bout nothin but making a man cum
both of them so preoccupied they didn't even see him pick up
the gun

At night he'd cry
cuz his daddy lied
told him he would be to get him
never showed or gave no reason why
and when his tears dried
he took a deep sigh
and silently wished that his daddy would die

She was never there
He knew it wasn't fair
but he'd managed to learn
to pretend not to care
It was all he could bare
cuz he'd never dare share
and give her any reason
to even pretend to care
When he knew deep inside

RECONCILIATION

she'd rather her legs in the air

They both blamed each other
Fault father then mother
and she'd rather complain
how he never did love her
and he'd shun her for constantly trying to uncover
the reason why he never officially cuffed her

Couldn't speak long enough to ever discover
The reason why their son stuttered
or how much that he suffered
She was more concerned that daddy's a sucker
and daddy just didn't feel like mommy starting to smother
together their behavior acted as ushers
guiding innocence out
guiding in a vicious motherfucker

At eleven years old
There'd come the crusher
when peer pressure kicked in
and the streets had a luster
and the lack of parenting showed
in his failure to muster
the reasoning required
to avoid the falls of the gutter

Without a curfew
or a guardian to hover
a few blocks away he stumbled upon a big brother
who introduced him to green leaves

MOOD SWINGIN

and small rocks of butter
Pancakes and syrup
he said they were others
and then there was H
the moneymaker
He said of them all
that she was the taker

Went over numbers
preyed on his blind trust
all it took was the little attention
that he craved so much
And it was understood
as long as there was never a blunder
then little man would be
his number one runner

With his new preoccupation
school took a backseat
his once safe haven
took the position of a snare drum
on an inconsistent back beat
instead of books in his backpack
he started to pack heat
Trap music ran through his veins
he was changing
adjusting to life on the backstreets

Whenever he showed signs
it was too easy to play both sides
his parents egos wouldn't allow them to cross check

RECONCILIATION

so he played them both times

All of the while his ego was growing
Living a private life
without anyone knowing,
Pockets on swole
ROI is ongoing
the little innocence maintained
was quickly eroding
but there would come the day
when everything started unfolding

See youngin was slippin
he started dippin into the green leaves
he was supposed to be pitchin
Money was missin
and he started bitchin
trying to recall the number of L's he had been hittin

His mama came in yelling
his daddy in tow
he was in for it there was no telling
but for what
he didn't know

They'd been to the school
where the record did show
that he had been marked absent
for 30 days in a row

Little to say

MOOD SWINGIN

cuz that was the least of his worries
he remained silent
patiently awaiting the moment they'd scurry
Had bigger fish to fry
so he personally wished that they'd hurry
so that he could deal with the emotions
that he was struggling to bury

Just like he figured
it wouldn't be long before they started to bicker
Pops said mom could stand be a little bit stricter
she walked away calling him a stupid ass nigga
And he could finally focus on his own big picture

Impatience grew
And instinctively he knew
That he'd have to move fast
If he was gonna push through
Listening to his parents yelling as the argument continued to
stew

Slipped out of his room and the house
pants with an extra sag
they'd barely noticed him leave
or how his left leg dragged

He was on a mission
both scared and sad
but in his situation
he didn't see what other choice he had

RECONCILIATION

Maybe he zigged when he should have zagged
but his destination seemed closer than the memory he had
target in focus
adrenaline on go
attitude atrocious
bust down with ammo
crept up unnoticed
piece cocked and he quickly outgrows
being the closest little man
to his one time hero
he raises it
aims and lets his thing go
hitting his target in the chest
three times in a row

Scurried off
like a thief in the night
nothing would be the same
he'd be playing a waiting game
and sanity
he'd probably never reclaim

Confusion set in
as he tried to think
he was threatened and stressed
finally realizing that he'd been hoodwinked

He wanted to be a kid
but was never allowed
and for that he became
a grown ass child

MOOD SWINGIN

his behavior a result
of the bullshit compiled
and his lack of ability to even beguile
his parents to care enough to mature and begin to reconcile

Exhausted, he stopped running
ducked into an alleyway
overwhelmed and consumed
by who he was becoming
slipping again
he didn't hear the footsteps drumming
closing in on him
as he released longing tears of wanting

Hands Up!
Was all that he heard them say
He was just 12 years old
trying to find a better way
I love you
that's all he wanted his parents to say
and if this is his right now
what will his life look like past today?
Hands up
they screamed again
and he raised his hands
but only to raise the gun to his chin
it was all he could stand
or the rest of his life lived boxed in
at an early age lived a life filled with sin
knew he'd be an urban legend
pulled the trigger

RECONCILIATION

**died instantly
on his face was a grin**

www.ingramcontent.com/pod-product-compliance
Lightning Source LLC
Chambersburg PA
CBHW062035120526
44592CB00036B/2139